Heart on the Mc

by Philip Sher

ISBN 978-1-291-61909-6

For Helen

Contents

Preface

Heart On the Mountain describes a vision of place, both literal and metaphoric, upon the land. When I speak of the land I mean both the intrinsic and extrinsic landscape and the boundless boundary between the two.

Mountains metaphorically embody the heart and occupy a central place in many ancient cultures. When we climb a mountain we do so to take in the breath taking views and to enjoy the broad horizon. In doing this we often find our perceptions alter or shift to take in the all encompassing vision. We return to the world refreshed and re-invigorated to re-engage with Life and our relationships with a more meaningful and embodied sense of purpose.

Just so, mountains abide in the surrounding landscape with their roots embedded in the earth. They have uplifted themselves but in doing so they immediately begin a slow inexorable return to the land through the erosive forces of wind and water, a geological cycle we can witness if we choose to see it.

I remember the long, difficult and painful task of learning to walk after my accident. At one point, exhausted from my efforts after an intensive physiotherapy session I wrote, 'how every step, every turn and every standing moment felt like an Everest.' Looking back after more than ten years of practice l wonder with no small degree of awe at the many steps l have taken, none of which l have taken for granted.

For many of those steps l found myself accompanied by some very kind and supportive people, far too numerous to name here. Each gave and shared a thousand kindness's that helped me on my way. I trust that I returned in kind the generous hearted attitude and embodiment of those values that go beyond words. I dedicate this book of poems to those who make helping, sharing and giving a credo in their lives.

These poems have enabled me to track my experience on this climb up and down the mountain of my recovery from that near fatal motorcycle accident. I survived but faced a immense struggle to return from the devastation of that impact.

I think poems find you at the right time and place for you to notice them. These poems appeared in moments when I least expected them, the flash of a kingfisher, the abyss of depression, a blossom rapturously illuminated in low golden sunlight. They have differing structures and forms, they don't all finish with a neat and tidy ending.

I like to think of them in the words of Kuno Meyer when he described the ancient celtic form of poetry in his introduction to the collection, Selections From Ancient Irish Poetry:

> It is a characteristic of these poems that in none of them do we get an elaborate or sustained description of a scene or scenery, but rather a succession of pictures and images which the poet, like an impressionist, calls up before us by light and skilful touches. Like the Japanese, the Celts were always quick to take an artistic hint; they avoid the obvious and the commonplace; the half-said thing to them is dearest.
> Meyer K. (1911, p.xii - xiii), Selections From Ancient Irish Poetry. London: Constable & Company Ltd.

By way of an introduction to the poems I have included a piece of writing I produced soon after discharge from hospital called, Broken Places. I wrote it to record the still raw experience of my accident and the thoughts I had while I lay on the road awaiting the arrival of the emergency services.

As I reflect on my journey of recovery and rehabilitation I think Life asks only that we live with loving kindness toward all things and most importantly that we love ourselves in the same way too. A Taoist and Confucian concept encapsulates this in a simple, yet complex term, Ren. Meaning on one level at least, that we all have a place in the world and that place acts as a covenant between all things.

It remains, as ever, for us as embodied beings to act consciously with Ren - loving kindness - to embrace our infinite potential for giving, sharing and supporting one another.

So, may the road rise before you and the wind be always at your back, and beauty fill your life with every breath.

Maybe, we will meet somewhere in the world.

Philip Sheridan

Broken Places

So, here I rest on the tarmac looking at the grey sky.

'I'm still alive.'

Luck, skill, providence, all it seems have conspired to keep me alive. How? I have just collided with a lorry. I see it as I regain control of my bike, albeit that I am drifting directly into a head on impact with it. I steer to avoid the fatal front end, the back tyre skidding over the tarmac. I accelerate as fast as I can to avoid the crunch of my soft body with so much hard steel.

Instead, I hit at an deflected angle into the front wheel on the drivers side of the cab. Then chaos. A swift change from going forwards to stopping instantly, then like a dog mauling a rag doll I'm spat back onto the ground. I hit the road so hard the force seems to expel every atom of air out of my body.

For a short while all comes to rest as my senses try to catch up. I have crashed.

'I'm still alive ... but for how long?'

A man with a moustache and tousled hair appears, he opens my visor and begins mouthing words. I'm in a world of numbness and silence. He takes off my sunglasses minus their ear pieces.

'Strange,' I think to myself.

'All right mate stay still an ambulance is on its way. I won't take your helmet off.'
'Well, at least he knows that.'
I feel sorry for him, he shakes like a leaf in the wind, he looks around and down unsure where to look.
'What's your name?' I ask as I take his hand in mine.
'Colin.'
'Hello Colin, I'm Phil.'

A woman walks over to ask if an ambulance has been called, she looks at me horrified.

'This can't be good.'

I begin to check myself. I try to wriggle my toes but only those in my left foot seem to respond. My right leg buzzes with white noise, I can't feel a thing and it won't move. I try my fingers and hands, then ever so gently my hips and shoulders, happily for now, I conclude I'm not paralysed.

Time ebbs and flows on a wave of peculiar sensations, the thump of my heart, the suck of air into my lungs, the crushing awareness of death. I hold Colin's hand, cool air on my exposed face, my vision restricted to the sky above me, all sound muffled by my helmet.

'The Police are here,' Colin says.

PC Edwards comes over and assures that an ambulance will arrive soon. He speaks with Colin off to one side. I hear Colin explain how he saw me round the corner slowly yet slipped into the path of his truck. He repeats his surprise as he watched me slowly disappear beneath him.

In this short interlude I begin a more thorough check of myself. I feel with my hands over my body and legs. Colin gently removes my hands from trying to reach down my right leg.

'Don't you worry, you're going to be OK,' he says.

I know that things don't look good. I want to see what has happened to me.

Eventually the paramedic team arrive and they commence a detailed examination of my injuries. They ask me questions as they feel around my body. After some time they decide we can remove my helmet. They unbuckle the strap and ever so carefully it slips from my head.

Freed from the constraints of my helmet I look around. To my left, I see the total wreck of my bike stripped of its bodywork, twisted forks, bent wheels, bits and pieces strewn across the road. My heart sinks, *'I've killed my bike.'*

As an oxygen mask is placed over my mouth I look down toward my legs. My right leg is bent and twisted in a most awkward way. Sticking five or six inches skyward from the back of my boot I see the pink de-fleshed bone of my tibia. I see smaller splinters of bone and I see a puddle of blood forming.

As I get loaded into the ambulance the pain begins to swell and I think to myself, *'Well if this can be fixed its going to need some kind of miracle, things are never going to be the same again, I'm probably going to lose my leg.'*

The journey to Scarborough Accident & Emergency takes an age, every twist, turn and bump shoots bolts of agony throughout my body. The paramedic sits beside me and stays in physical contact with me all the way.

'Stay with me son,' he says, 'we can't go too fast because of your injuries, hold on for me.'

I reply that I will, but I know from the way he looks at me that he doesn't think I will.

'Why did I choose such an exposed and lonely place to crash.'

I arrive at Scarborough Hospital and from the calm of the ambulance I enter into a throng of bodies at the double doors. I felt at ease in the ambulance, I felt happy to die and had laid quietly content with the prospect.

As I go through the doors of A&E I realise all these people have other priorities than to simply let me die. I smile and say, 'hello.' They seem a little surprised that I can answer their questions so cogently. With much sighing, whispers and exclamations, polaroids are taken for posterity.

Mobile X-ray equipment moves into place to irradiate me from head to foot. I hurt so much. A nurse takes my hand. That touch felt so important, to hold and to be held. It anchors me to the possibility that I might still live. It gives me hope that I might hold hands intimately again.

The Consultant continues to question me as another nurse cuts my leathers and boots from my legs.

'Where does it hurt? Did I lose consciousness at any point? How much pain am I in?'

It feels like I have fallen into an ocean of pain. The consultant explains that they need to turn my foot around. I take deep steady breaths and slip into Entanox land. Dimly, distantly, I hear the consultant say, 'standby everyone,' as my shoulders, arms and hips held down by strong hands restrain me as they pull and rotate my foot back to its normal position.

As the flood gates open a doctor with a consoling expression on his face shows me a consent form to which I need to give next of kin. He explains to me what they have found, I catch fragments as I try to remember telephone numbers for my family and friends. I feel overwhelmed by the grave decision I now face.

He says, 'Do you understand that your right leg is so damaged that we may well need to amputate? We will do our best, but to be honest it's worse than anything I've seen. I've worked in Bosnia treating land mine injuries.'

I want to cry at that point. I want to close my eyes, open them and all will be OK. Instead, I take a deep breath and reach for some strength heretofore never needed until now.

'Well,' I say, 'if it has to come off then take it off, but I would prefer if you could try and save it.' He seems to agree while he hands me a pen and the consent form.

So, I signed my leg away and crossed a threshold. I did so with the knowledge that if I survived the surgery I would awake to an unknown becoming.

*   *   *

Heart on the Mountain

Made of Beauty

Made of land
Of sky
Of sun, moon and stars.

Made of wind,
Of cloud
Of mist, rain and snow.

Made of trees,
Of flowers
Of all things green.

Made of flesh,
Of bone
Of blood, skin and nerve.

Made of love,
Of heart
Of thought, word and deed.

Made of beauty,
Of spirit
Of warp, weft and weave.

All things
Made beautiful.

Sin

Have I sinned
Against life?

Have I crossed
The bounds,
Of nature's modesty?

Have I taken
For granted,
The gift of living?

Have I stretched
The threads
Of necessity?

I have sat
Days of grief and mourning.

Blossom

O my soul
To keep in peace,
Open the petals of my heart,
A blossom to the sun.

Cleave my roots in the earth,
Let the wind wash over me,
Let me drink my fill
Of loving rain.

Take care of my still tender wounds,
Rest those broken places,
Where bones and flesh
Have healed.

Let me abide
In the quiet presence
Of the land and sky.

Edge

Standing at the edge
I cried for death,

But death did not come.

I wept for life
But life replied,

So.

Rest

At the heart of life
Rests a stillness,

A place where we
Receive absolution,

A space opens within
And our hearts unfurl.

Wind blows through a hollow bone
White and dry,

A resonance
Forever keens remembrance.

Sifting

I live within an inner space,
The other side of the mirror.

Light does not penetrate here.

Looking out
From interior darkness,
Only silence listens.

In the depths of feeling,
Moved by echoes of a past belonging,
Another way beckons.

Through the mill,
Ground to dust,
Of who and what I had become
Has gone.

A finer thing remains.

Definition

You want me to be like you,
Not different.

Not remind you that life
Is contingent,
To make you feel
Uncomfortable in your skin.

Not remind you that wholeness
Is not physical,
But the great invisible.

Not remind you that the body
Does not define,
The boundary of self.

Not remind you that all
That is material,
Is not being.

You want me to be like you,
But I'm not.

Release

Let the arrow go
In one heart beat of the bow,

Returning home

Still.

Stories

We become the stories
We hear,
We become the stories
We tell.

Do the stories
You hear
Have their roots
In the earth?

Do the stories
You tell
Return you
To the people?

Do the stories
You feel
Embrace you
With love?

Reflections

Sun struck flecks of light,

Silver and brilliant white
Against gunmetal clouds,

Seagulls!

They Who Came

Life has its own urgency.
When life gets pushed to the edge of death,
Then a company of characters come forth
To take on the challenge of perpetuating
Life's love of living.

Primal in essence
They abide within the recesses of our ancient ancestral
memories,
Long buried under sophisticated modernity,
Laying dormant,
Nullified by comfort and ease.

Only when the imperative demands
Do they awaken
And remember themselves upon the earth;
As principals of life,
They have no concern for our petty conceptual personalities.

They come as heroes
Of a time long past,
Where the bounds of life from death
Had not become so distinct,
Their only primacy, to prevail in the face of adversity.

Once they have answered the call,
Shaken the dust from their armour
And taken up their arms,
They will dutifully abide
As a honour guard to our integrity.

Survivor
Will do anything to stay alive
At any cost,
Summoning every last fibre of being
To stay alive.

Terror
Stares into the abyss
Realises your ending,
Your complete annihilation.
Absence declares the presence of death.

Grief
Sobbing with sadness
For the loss of becoming.
Transfiguring hurt with
The loving rain of care.

Innocence
Opening the heart
To the possibility of renewal.
To smile and accept
The grace of life.

Valour
Determines to live
Without mediocrity
With a diamond hard
Bright spirit.

Jigsaw

A piece
Placed, played
One piece
At a time.

A step
Here, there
One step
At a time.

A story
Told, said
One word
At a time.

Grip

Death took hold of me
And said,

'You're alive!'

Dare

I dare you
To drop out of your head
And live in your heart instead.

I dare you
To drop further,
To leap from your heart
And land on the earth.

I dare you
To lay down in the sun
Heavy as a sleeping dog.

I dare you
To rest your soul,
Abate the listless worries of your mind
And listen to a greater voice instead.

Changeling

I feel
Good about my life,

An ever changing flow
Of weather.

I feel no one definition of self,
A plurality of thought,

A republic of mind.

Return

Before your threshold
I meet you,

Standing at the welcome
Of your hearth,

And in the presence of you
I find the ground,

To return to the fire place
Where love is kindled,

And burns bright
In the belonging,

Of one to another.

Crack

From the crucible
Forged in fire
Tempered in water
Polished on stone
A flower cracks the rock.

Run

I find my rhythm
In the land,
Join with it
And find my ease in the world.

I extend my body,
My hearts tempo
Into my limbs,

And remember myself
Whole again.

Care

A poem arrives
All fresh and raw,
Senses tingling,
Eyes unblinking.

Do you catch it,
Clasp it in your arms,
Bring it close
To your heart,

Nurture the potential
It carries,
Not demand its justification,
But let it alone.

Let it ease into life,
Stretch out
And rest awhile,
Let it find its feet,

Grow grass between
Its toes,
Learn to dance
With grace and poise,

Find its own tune,
That just might
Remind you of the one
You once had at birth.

Take care then,
Not to tread
On the heads of poems,
Babes or flowers.

Pass

I am small
Within this landscape.

Yet my thoughts,
If I allow, can range
Beyond the horizon.

Reach back
To thoughts conceived
In heads and hearts
Just like mine.

That felt this wind,
this sunshine, this ground.

That spoke
Of what might become,
Of what had happened.

I am not alone then,
I am immersed

In this land,
In a sea of thought,
Of feeling.

Of countless others,
Who live,
Or did live.

Of those who will come,
After I have passed.

Offspring

She abides
In hare and hound

Stride for stride
Life bound

Dew washed feet
Earth pound

Soft underbellies
Bellow misty
Dissipating breath

Offspring of the ground.

Wayfarer

So, without any effort
Let the earth carry you.

Without force or contention,
Leave everything to work naturally.

Without contriving plans
Allow all to unfold as it will.

Abide with patience
The earth can only carry you,

One day at a time.

Biography

Philip Sheridan (b. 1963) draws his inspiration from the deep elemental presence of the land. He asserts a landscape not of wilderness, not one absent of human life but rather the compelling need to remember ourselves and our relationship to the land.

Philip hitchhiked around the USA, Canada, Mexico and Australia when he finished school at 18. On his return to Britain he worked in hotel and catering, as a freelance photographer, and children's therapist, among other things.

Philip lost his right leg below the knee in a near fatal motorcycle accident on Friday 13th September 2002. He suffered horrific injuries to his legs, arms, and head, including the amputation of his right leg below the knee. He sustained his recovery by adapting and mastering his many years of practise in the martial arts and went on to become an accomplished rock climber.

A final operation in early 2010 to remove the eleven metal screws and plate from his right femur enabled him to run again after almost nine years of pain and severe discomfort. After running on a prosthetic leg designed for walking for 8 months Philip received a 'blade' running leg as recognition of his hard work and dedication.

Inspired he set himself the challenge on the 10th anniversary of his accident in 2012 to run the Dales Way long distance trail, over 80 miles / 130km in three days, raising over £2000 for the charities, Martin House Children's Hospice, Mind, Combat Stress, and Survival International.

As well as the physical effort and discomfort his injuries exact upon his body, Philip suffers with the debilitating affects of Post Traumatic Stress and Depression. Running within the landscape has proved a beneficial therapy both physically and emotionally.

Philip drew upon the techniques he used in his therapeutic work with traumatised children to help himself. Creative writing became an important medium of reflection. It help him to grasp the enormity of surviving significant trauma and ameliorate the transition from an able bodied life to one of impairment and disability.

Philip speaks and lectures as an inspirational expert patient on the lived experience of surviving significant trauma, recovery and rehabilitaion. He works as a Simulated Patient at the University of Leeds Institute of Medical Education and offers consultation on the patient clinician relationship, patient involvement and communication with patients.

He talks about widening his horizons when he speaks and presents. Taking ownership, engaging with opportunity, participating in dialogue, building relationships, giving back and paying forward, all underpinned with a deep well of appreciation and gratitude. Philip has built his recovery on the foundation of these themes and values.

'Just because something seems impossible today, doesn't mean it won't become possible tomorrow.'

www.philip-sheridan.com

Printed in Great Britain
by Amazon